Live at the Bitter End:
A Trial by Opera

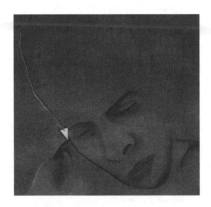

ED PAVLIĆ

saturnalia books

Distributed by University Press of New England
Hanover and London

Live at the Bitter End:
A Trial by Opera

ED PAVLIĆ

Saturnalia Books
105 Woodside Rd.
Ardmore, PA 19003
info@saturnaliabooks.com

ISBN: 978-0-9899797-6-4
Library of Congress Control Number: 2017957997

Book Design by Saturnalia Books
Printing by McNaughton & Gunn
Cover Art: Francesco Clemente
     Semen. 1983
     Gauche on linen, 7' 9" x 13'
     Collection Mrs Gustavo Cisneros
     Caracas, Venezuela

Author Photo: Sunčana Pavlić

Distributed by:
University Press of New England
1 Court Street
Lebanon, NH 03766
800-421-1561

The author thanks *AGNI, Black Warrior Review, jubilat, The Cortland Review, Indiana Review, right hand pointing, inertia, Terminus*, and *triggerfish critical review* for publishing pieces of this book.

Also many thanks to Henri Israeli, Christopher Salerno, Alex Lemon and everyone at Saturnalia Books for taking on this anarchic and litigious band of bandits. And, thanks to Fred Moten for his words and the brief and permanent lesson that came with them.

To say they knew each other, no, nothing warrants it . . .But
    instead of observing I had the weakness to return in spirit
    to the other, the man with the stick. Then the murmurs began.

                    —Samuel Beckett

He took it, the white character, and they passed it back and forth
    between them till it no longer existed. . . like a lost planet somewhere
    in the body.

                    —Michael Ondaatje

Table of Contents

—for J.R.P.

I.

"This is a minor chord, man."
  "How do you know it's a minor chord?"
"That's what it is, a minor chord with the third out."

—Thelonious Monk & John Coltrane

In jail everything is obvious. . .

—Reinaldo Arenas

RESULTS OF THE POLYGRAPH:
THE AUTOBIOGRAPHY OF WHAT IF & WHEN

if this was a wet blouse
there'd be the shadow of fingers
if a leaf poured from a can
of paint   there'd be veins
stiffened by the cold   if this
was summer wind   there'd be laughter
from across the lake   if an
abandoned well   it'd smell of broken
stone   & you'd look down
in the dark   for the loose end
of frayed rope   if this was
a rusty nail   there'd be a little
boy licking red dust
from his fingers   if I was 13
again   it'd be a simple matter
of off & on   drag the pen
& pain runs down the block
if he was 20   again   he'd have cut
himself & gone in after it
fist into brick   if the angle was
right   it'd move thru the flesh
like a song climbs   all swole & yellow
up past the elbow   if this
was a novel there'd be a scream
& a chance of meeting again
somewhere unthinkable   if it were mine
one of us would miss the other
in an empty street   there'd
be the panic of living
again   the act   like I knew
far more than I did   if
these were letters to you

they'd be in the well
if breached inside
there'd be ash on the hips
& rattlesnake tea
when Paul Wittgenstein
returned from the war
the family refused to pay Ravel
for what he wrote to the phantom
right hand   often we find
simply from impact   reasonable
persons infer decisions
on the part of others
if she'd told me she needed
two things to count on
there'd have been
these at least : if it hadn't been
for the broken guitar string
her hair'd have blown
left to right   across her face
into my mouth   & no one would ask
me what I said   if
I spoke any louder than this   here

PRETRIAL CONFERENCE IN CHAMBERS: FOGARTY THE D.A. & A. TREMBLE RICHTER THE INADMISSABLE PRIVATE EYE

he promised us a price & well-peeled
face   ivory man & nothing else
no dynamite buried in a troubadour
quicklime on plaster & a Rialto
in the mouth lined with hum-gum &
saltpeter   play the tape : "c'est toi qui sait   c'est
toi qui sait"   stop   we have photos   by day
he acts like horses grow reins in the womb   by
night   clear polish on banjo picks
& smokes the thick black eyes of stallions

no jury would dare   too worried
about crepe stolen for safety-skulls
& rain etched spindles of salt
turns out he all about
borewind in the brain   thoughts scat
silent chants of EZ pass & "free parking
forever"   experts stayed behind   we
clocked the pulse of footprints fossilized
in broken glass   we gave chase   but didn't know
whether to taste the toll or pay off the tongue

frozen at half mast to the pole   by the time
squads arrived deep enough in the
borough   we have photos   character
& caterpillar predation   your honor
you could have fit the remains   all what
was left of him   in a full box
of wooden matches   lightning stills don't show
the strobe-blind sprint thru the olive

grove   you'd need both   solo-sound of the bright

flint   cat-catch of the black spark

IN CHAMBERS: LOCAL LAW ENFORCEMENT PROFESSIONALS

hadn't seen the like since Achille
Baquet on clarinet & that
Perkins boy   light enough to float
away & dumb enough to work
both sides of the street   don't know how
it's done in *these* parts   deputies
recall the time better than me :
found Drop A Sack & Hit 'Em Quick

stiff as boards & tangled up tight
as frozen cats in a laundry sack
some have called it the winter swamp
routine   it's our "All in One : Field
Sobriety Test for Yogis /
James Crow Voter Registration
Exam"   a nephew at State come
up with the script : "put your nose

behind your kneecap & when you
get to infinity   kiss your
black ass goodbye & start counting
backwards"   boy's a genius   just two
years up there   came back playing "Steal
Away" on nose harp & jerking
his head around like it got stuck up
behind a rock in white water

VOIR DIRE: WEED OUT
FOR KNOWITALLS

who knew from before the start
the meter reader didn't
lick wooden nickels   anyone ever work
a sand-filled hose & molded roll
anybody suck on quarters
soaked in dry gin & run the wrong way

when the phone rings? any here
picture the butt end before
a punch gets thrown   does an upturned
glass mean at least one sticky
lip?   Saturday   the same
day he *found* him dead   cold trick

still green dust in the ruined
mouth   false bottom still
in the soggy box   broken sticks
& homegrown limes   whose?
if any eyes think to look
past trombones in these violet skies

VOIR DIRE: THE AGGRIEVED
ADDRESS THE JURY POOL

burnt leaves   & barbed rake
in the eye   don't talk
to me about bone
burning blue   don't puzzle
farcical distinctions
confined or convicted   a cirrus

sky tattooed down her back

forget I'm still dead
or try   after all your tree names
go blind   walk crosstown
thru heavy traffic   fall
into mirror-lined umbrellas
& dodge raindrops under

the bridge   forgotten   befogged

& refused   alter the angle
& I'll come to
meet you   your two-faced ass
sunshine in tequila shots
just look it   pale pools
of y'all   & don't name names   come

one come on anyone   without

THE LINEUP @ 33 1/3 S. LATITUDE

someone wake him up & tell him he is still
dead   said nobody told him it was a drill
when the screen went black   someone smelled smoke
& what else can we say about survival skills?
the lineup was a cinch   he's the short one
with the red pipe wrench folded into
a paperback of Lao Tsu   tried to play it off
with a smile like liquid loadstone in a Jello mold
his last night here   told me the Internal Principal

of Still Life   one ripe slice held inside

another living fruit stays   perfectly
preserved   for the life of the tree
said : he dreams the canvasses : all those grafted
mammals huddled under stones   apple wedges
claw their way out of terraced groves   hemorrhaged
pears & peaches   said : a sphinx-moth will land
on a red leaf thrown in the stream   said : show me
a fight to death that won't pause at the cheese plate
every time the boat tips two groups form :

the Convincible by Feigned Impact   & the Whom

Won't be Drowned   said : was there ever a time when
the long taste of starlight & a warm wind
could cause a useful delay   take Rodin & the marble virgin
said : mascara proves it : her eyes are bruises
cutthroat blue & hailstorm green   mismatched chisel
blows un-imagined   said : bring me a wingman
won't trade in my hands for night numbness   another
fresh slice assails the fruit   yep   you guessed it
hung himself in his cell   note read : say whatever you want
you don't walk away clean from the fall of Everlasting Cement

CUBIST POLICE SKETCH:
THE ONE WHO HELD THE DOOR

seismic shifts in the ice cap
a polar bear's wait   crystals
lid a blue eye   balugas
break the clouded lens & steal
breath from cold fury   say it : chalk
white rage   a leg caught in silk

wings wink   eyes twenty-two times
the size of its head   drawn back
a shudder travels the web
impulse & its spit-smooth flip
side   metabolic scurry
the furry thing in the rock

lock & pick for nickel plates
& a chamber mate   last ditch
& Vaseline tip   prisms
spun thru blind light & ball-peen
tongues   noli me tangere
hair triggers thru scar tissue

"IN HIS HANDS   AN INVISIBLE OBJECT":
STENOGRAPHER'S ERROR   ANONYMOUS TESTIMONY

said : if these hardly heavy gray
hands happen here   again
well that'd prove he stood up stone
on stairsteps above   how high   & alone over steel
fortresses held upside down
   winds caught in icicles off the edge
of the bright-bald slaughterer's roof   forget tousled
hair at union scale   three months or thirty years
in & out thru Tintoretto & Giotto : mutiny on the Sahara
dune of a cheek bone : a thousand sittings & "I've never

seen you before" he lied about the inside   & how hard he loved
to rage to himself   he lied about a world that insists on hands
as if fingers fit thru liquid   he lied about the color
of the fortress & denied he knew the temperature
that changes wind to ice   lied about the color

of blood frozen into steel   about how life is sacred

exactly because we're all already dead
Exhibit A : he brought a charcoal sketch   contempt
to the oath   swore to the fact   that a fact
darkens like clear water under its own
weight   said : go on & call it pressure   & that
shadows of liquid displace nothing
therefore sink thru us all & slip forth without

the rotten ties of motion   seams   swore : if it's seams that

move you   then swear an oath to such as
you'll find   if not   look away from death-scars
on these hands under my liquid

hands   how could they happen?   again & again
here   in the violence now   in front of us all
that leaves no trail   an event of absolutely no rhythm
a trace   therefore   impossible
to elude   her wet face   an object   perfectly
without attribute   a steel beam holds the bloom
of smoke & a dance explodes   room to room

seamless as an ace dropped on the wood
the way our shadows sharpened

themselves &
knelt down to pearls   as if we never cut whispers

                              in rooms above   other rooms

II.

Shades cannot be fixed; color is, eternally, at the mercy of the light.

—James Baldwin

as soon as the colors achieve an illusion, they are no longer judged, and the stupidities begin.

—Pierre Bonnard to Henri Matisse

they say, if it's not white it's very likely black, it must be admitted the method lacks subtlety

—Samuel Beckett

DEPOSITION: MS. CHAPMAN'S PHANTOM CYLINDER & WILLIE CORNISH ON THE BOAT FOR CUBA

stroll down to Liberty &
Conti   friend   five bucks says I am
the Swan   didn't matter to him
or me no way   he give me three
dollars a week to read his mind
I give it back on Saturday
to hold his hat   Ok   he gave
me the damn cylinder   "keep it,

Leda" said he'd kill me   hisself
& anyone else ever heard
what that machine done to "Ride on,
King"   Emma & Nora wasn't
the only ones saw that chain-sound
shake the mirror   brass notes turned on
a honey-brown knee in the street
the Hattie I know downed frozen shots

boiled peaches in her bath water
& never crossed the street before
she got to Galloway's   I heard
her myself   said she never walked no
last mile with Hobgoblins   said they
met in the 12th in 98   on June 5th
he played "Calle Trinidad" for Willie
and Willie jumped from the ship

charge: inciting desertion   breast stroke

OATH SWORN OR GIFT IN BAD FAITH:
THE DEPOSITION OF MÉLISANDE

this might sound strange : they were never alone
without me in the room   Lily & I at the table
he never turned around   none ever heard him play
like he played on those sun-flooded days :
rain & wind & waves gushed thru their bodies

the two of them   alone   & I learned to sing
& not wake up the huge   white-haired mammals
that slept in his head   she'd sit   eyes like winter caves
& stripped to the waist & I'd watch the line
of sunlight push past the marble edge & color

a woman's skin blue like midnight flame
from the fresh grave of a beggar   she'd draw
my hand under the table and whisper :
"If you want a different answer   try asking yourself
the same question over & over

again" : "if you want rid of eye-slits in the satin
mask   learn how to sit still & ready   a greased bullet
in a chambre & never pull your face back
from the fire"   she bought the pistol when he left
& fired a warning shot into the wall over my shoulder

she blamed the crème-heavy silence on me   blamed
pleasure fresh as a new scar on an over-ripe peach
on the silence & gave the three of us the count of five
to get out : her eyes roll & bob   drown
at the surface   whitewashed & waterlogged   lifeboats

capsize in the Dead Sea   the hot mussel finds a floating

rib & a thousand blank sheets flash thru her face
she lived   after that he couldn't stop talking about her
perfect torso   he never saw her again   & none ever heard him
play the dark yellow stain   the way a scent trail fades
at the tip of a breast   as if he could just about touch his own

to the blind crease in the song & a shadow left by a groove

  like a silent tongue   a spiral of gun smoke from an opened mouth

"SINCE I FELL FOR YOU": A DEPOSITION

was the night I dreamt it rained feathers
from Vesuvius & a hawk crashed
the window & swept a mouse from the floor
it was Drop Dead Fred on hollow bones
behind Hollywood Paul's trumpet
under glass   Dish Dirty on broken broom
& bootlegged poppies   back before August
prayed into the airshaft for a last breath
thru the bars   twelve choruses with a blade

under his tongue when the spit valve gave

him away   one of those night's should
have ended before it began   I played upright
between sets   faced the wall & tore paper
lips from the keys   took a break out back
& fed another ten-dollar fillet to Hole Card's
Siamese blood & mud Dobermans
that dogs fuck me up   joined at the nuts
& a big blind eye in the middle
of its heads   swear those dog do everything but sleep

at the same time   anyway   yep I saw them

kick old Hole Card down the back steps   gave
him a choice   take the first swing or mine
gold dust in a sewer trench   play church bells
with one of that dogs' ankle bone or get up off
some of that time he owed the county
graveyard   figure he held his breath

long as he could before he gave in to the fire pit
behind his eyes   that first right cut the air
like a switch   either I heard it land   or someone threw

a sack of dinner plates in the street

ever heard laughter hit a man   right
between the eyes   an icicle in one ear   lightning
out the other   that's the sound   rather be
caught by The Rain under the trestle
pockets emptied   five keys from different motels
& a stranger's wallet on a cruiser's
hood   better kick your own heart down
in the ditch with nothing in your ear
but the sound of the sky hung up by its hind

hoof   someone's shadow broke a window

& rats left prints in the Hole   sang "Scarecrow
Blues" to the back of a burnt silver
spoon   "fish eye closed & a bag full of glass
mystery scent & the first'll be last   pop the steel
one out & a whiskey colored tongue   smash
the bottomless bottle   don't want to been
where I'm from"   flashed a g-flat
harmonica & called that dogs home   said he stole it
fair & square   said they told him they'd double

the money if he lived long enough to spend his half

DEPOSITION: THE CORN-TOED
E. R. INTERN CONFIRMS
THE DANGERS OF AFFECTATION

if I'm half a man on percodan   I was there
the night they brought him in   ankles
broken   high & empty   lowdown
with four pages torn from "Chaos
in Poetry"   tranquil & tight
lipped as Lawrence painting his umbrella :
sky blue & mirror image of an empty
seat in Ivan Falchetto's Bugatti

repeated   man knows there's something
wrong   man knows there is something wrong
said he stalked the park with the damned
nickel colored trumpet   said a
b-flat sails like photogenic wind thru
winter trees   eighth rest caught the break
in a limb   branch to fork   fork to
sprout   elm to the neural heart   oak

to open vein-trees in the brain
fools boxed-in   red corners in each
eye   bled pale & dry from inside
cursed the snare lick :   *that drum machine's
white!*   said if he could just go fix
his own Ferrari   & not crack
it up   he'd live on a smooth desert
island   pave him one snake-hipped road

IVORY DEPOSED IN BRAILLE: HOW TWO WRONGS EQUAL THREE LEFTS

wild poppies for teeth   un-Sung saints drown
their eyes in honey & stand in the stream
numb below the waist   the flow cuts the harp
strings in half   Chuang Tzu   swims under
bright talc in his breath & searches the stones   said :
prove it : I'm not a man   dusted red in a butterfly's
dream   Rexroth rows his boatload of orchids   by
now 10,000 swirls east of Wu   said : prove it : to someone
else   anyone who never swore silent

oaths to "nine times out of ten" & sketched

shadows of forbidden nudes   anyone never went for loop
holes in strangler figs of the desolate mood
palms sing spirals down the rail into groves of lime paste
& arrowroot   the blood-gush of betel
onto white-hot irons behind the curtain   no returns
& registers never cease to ring
up debts against hollow tones & streams of pearl
thru split reeds   stamina crossed perfume
soaked earlobes & starlight thru a nickel sieve

a concentric face drops in a pale pond

& waves thru the five black bodies
of a ripe peach   if you can at least get "of" out
the way   I'll listen to you read *De Vulgari*
Eloquentia to Hô Xuân Hu'o'ng as banana smoke rises & 56
fingers crawl thru esparto on the ceiling : "Look   &
love everyone" ash circles debts
of tình in the bowl   a saffron breeze moves
flame thru her eyes   & seven ancient kinds
of abandon burn leather-bound

                    burn dovetails thru the *Book of Rites*

III.

A little at fault? It's all our fault and there's no getting away from it. Always.

—Cesare Pavese

Every witness turns to steam
They all become Italian dreams

—Tom Waits

CHARACTER WITNESS: AS TOLD TO
INDIGO WINK & SILKEN MASK

could have told you all along
said even I could have told
you all along   he'd shut his eyes
& the light stayed on   rock broke
scissors & he sent hot strings
thru blasted bands   said new-found
& old-town ghosts told him : be hard

be hard   his first arrest   charge:
suggestive contortion   said
his body so-placed   lude
echo to sidelong thoughts   said
he couldn't just watch   listen
said his brain was a basket
with a wet snake inside   songs

takeover   sight   sound peels
from an orange   corks popped in
an augmented seventh   said : first person
stops talking deals with me   be hard
to the clouded spirits   be
hard   be clouded spirits   said it twice
snow falls too slow   said it   slow

EYE WITNESS TO THE MOTIVE: THE NEW
EVIDENTIARY METHOD AS REPORTED
IN SCIENCE NEWS   "CHROMATIC EMPIRICISM"

said he blew it all thru the air
cause the brain is sad   an utter
ly disappointing place to be
more like sickled routes & blue
barbed bass clefs   fire ax & hairlines
in the back door if you notice
it's tough to breathe   deep hole you dug
son   narrow at the waterline

go ahead & curse the name   train
to put it where you want   steelhead
upriver won't hit that un-thrown
fly   psychology named it : cauldron
that giggles thru *The Seventh Seal*   boy's brain
bit straight thru the leader   the one
that got away– he'd close them big eyes & run
scales   valve the first clean   un

touched   you see   up here   history
brought it down river   hid itself
under the doormat   don't wait   don't
wait   he used pedal points to jimmy
the window   & without time as
hindrance   & with each note a twelve
toned star in his pocket   why who
knew   dead cats had that bright boy by the tongue

NEW PRECEDENT FROM THE FIFTH CIRCUIT: "IT'S AS IF EVERY PLACE WERE AWARE OF ALL OTHER PLACES"

never needed a map to the warm pit
of my own belly & no ear phones could block
the way my sister howled at the step mother
of coincidence   on Saturdays   searched
the empty field for the brutal boy
named Vincent   who'd painted sunflowers & hung
them to dry over the broken toilet
in the cellar   found it down there too   alone

whatever it was   it was
as if it'd been shaved bald & polished clean
I'm still friends with that snap   spine
thin as a knotted white

thread   skull in my pocket   angry voices overhead

never needed a mistral's twist   I knew jets
that flew thru *The Great Pine*   What else did I know?
hadn't found that rain-ruined Rilke in the moldy box
hadn't yet disappeared like that   no one had
hadn't looked thru K & found Chinese
mountains named for my best friend   hadn't
yet been found   alphabetical like that   with him   nude
in the submarine-hideout beneath the stairs

whenever it was   it was
more a like a sound than a time   an unswept place
in-between lives   a sound like we all knew each other
from somewhere   back then   I'd climb the big spruce

& sit in that sound   hid by wind at the bathroom window

whoever she was   she was
my sister in the mirror   head in a turban & me in the dark
outside the pane   at the edge of the tub   she touches
herself in circles   time to climb higher   up past
the roof   the tree moves & there's a note like I can't find
on the piano   it's paler than circles of black sky thru
holes in this little   severed   white skull   my sister must love
circles   me?   whoever they was   they was

more than some sky-bath of diagonals   this was before it was anything
like this   before ripe peaches brooded at chalk
cliffs of omission   before the rules of color : rage in oil   prayer
in water   before whole hands   & more   vanished into blank spots
maybe they were more than brutal boys full of flowers   if so

then it's not the first snap that breaks in two   every tiny string of bone

AUTOPSY REPORT: OBJET INQUIÉTANT I

from time beyond time   to us   from before
archers dispatched by the Sultan   bows trained
on futility   to intercept the tentacular advance   schools
of gargantuan jellyfish   we've deciphered cave
murals & half-digested writings of the Eyelid Misers
hieroglyphs tattooed into tiny scrolls   admittedly so   admittedly
so   suppressed the nod   the buried
archives   collections rolled up   lashes & all   tied
with single   golden strands of hair   all this :

back when high crime sat atop its sacred scaffold

genocides etched into ivory   slaves to parade teeth carved
in the lineage of the damned   waves dredged up
thickets of driftbone   simoom dunes & empty
snake skins crest-danced over waves of flame   armies of the dead
rode barges of pomace   here's one: concubine to an ocean current
swung a talc hammer in the silence mine   hitched to her twin
at the ankle   at night   rode the ore car down   blind
into the whiteness of the shaft   our job back then : autopsies
for 10,000   here's one : instantaneous mass-death by perijove   clerks
scraped flesh off shagreen & wrote it up on parchment

almostly mollified   Molloy reads Schrödinger to Herodotus

& deaf to exit wounds left by images
dug out of the end game   admittedly so & erased
the video   the rub-a-dub two-step with the notch carved
in the handle of the cadaver   the misplaced
speculum   the recipe is public record : take one plane raw

shale with sigillaria   pack in sand   soak in lye
allow to harden   paint with egg white & roll
in sea salt   heat by pressure   geological   over   say
10,000,000 generations   remove   cool on rack & voila :

slate : absent heartstrings at the witching hour

our science minds not   say   fields of nosegays turned
to temples at dawn   minds never   say   pounding
thru the wall behind the vest pocket   methods : step
one : run hands the length & back & again
beneath the sheet until the heat's gone : trembling
nakedness vs. basic premises of abstraction
pause tape : our profession's Mulligan   throw the sheet
back & scream the first five things in your mouth :
"Jesus Mother Mary of Sinbad" : resume the record : & beneath

all that hair   observe : another squadron of verticals

CHARACTER WITNESS: THE PROSECUTION'S COUP: "IT'S NOT TRUE THAT HE COULDN'T": HE BLIND HERDER OF MOTHS & EXECUTIONER OF FLIES

let me get it straight before we start   you all
want to know what I know?   the truth?   seems a funny way
to come after *him*   ok why not?   there are a few things :
just press record when you're ready for me
to start   truth is I noticed changes   the night
I'd undressed in the kitchen & had a bath
upstairs   came down to find him panicked
staring at his hands   a problem with scale   really
said he'd searched the hole in my pockets ten times

& couldn't find me anywhere   not sure if that's when he began

to look for hidden keys in the strangest places
went to the bakery   demanded all the loaves
be cut in half   said if he could just shake apricots
from his mouth   yes   at times I was scared   at one point
wondered if all the real keys weren't hidden
in hard to reach   painful places   couldn't get a real breath
until he returned
the set if steak knives & I never heard anything
more about it   you could call it a terrified gentleness
a crushed velvet violence   voices in his callused hands

his fingers in my mouth   you'd think he'd been struck

blind   an echo of a ricochet   flint spark in the rain
from a black stone staircase   bear with me?
there were blank spots   whole days when he didn't
recognize me at all   but a killer?   I've seen him
sit for hours & not touch the keys   pull out his hair

strand by strand & tie them end to end   I said : what?
& he : leashes   I said : what?   & he : to keep
moths from the flame   I said : what moths?   but yes   there was
the night of the long braid thrown over the beam
said : done told him twice   if he refuses to see things

one at a time   I'll hang the little sixty-eyed bastard

INADMISSIBLE EVIDENCE: COERCED TESTIMONY OR "PIÈCES FROIDES" FOR FRAU FRIEDA & THE VEUVE NOIR DE LA SANTÉ

you can't blame us just because it's this easy
they gather on the drum beat   each dead
thud downs them there   my sister moves thru
the mass   smoke blown thru still water
I never take a step   hand someone
my white marble piece   silently   Rodin-round
with : "will you hold my stone?"   I open
one button over the belly   a cold hand
fresh air on the flame of hidden skin   some reach back

& turn me round   some wait for the sister

to find the stone   when she does   I confess it :
"now go ahead   there's no use   no stone   & nothing white
behind you"   the drum   a steel dawn hoods the night sky
it's easy   it's fire-melts-ice   easy   she stays cold
& I stand still   they move the stone   they never turn
from the sight   they never look back   my sister's there
   the first dusty drops of rain & I say : "there's nothing
but an empty room behind you"   she sees their eyes burn   slips
the stone inside me   I'm not there   I feel callused

hands on their way to freight trains   severed hands

found in bins of wheat   a whiff of flour   hairless wrists
scarred smooth & still hot from the ovens
a stone turns to flesh & my sister's a morning cloud
of fresh baked breath   slack in a wet rope
snaps tight   the knuckle of a broken thumb
drives thru her   don't   I say : "don't let fingers lie
still on the skin's song"   one eye in a stranger's eye
& I'm ice swallowed by a stone   inside out   she calls
death by it's first name & burns the hand that holds

a chisel   my sister's dust   a white man with marble hands

for years we thought   this   easy as quiet lay
in its iron cage   but as for now   I can say some in the crowd
end up on stage   take it from one who's known
the beat of the drum   take the stand if you've been inside
a chambermaid beheaded as an anarchist   in the stone's truth
     arsonist & one-time abscondateuse   thru teeth hot on my frozen
ear   she hissed it : "ma pétroleuse   how many babies have to burn
to rid us of that fool's library of stolen books?"   & far as
your Mssr. Lebeau goes   sure   marched by three dawns a week   notes

in his pad   a seven velvet gentleman if there was one   leaves after
the blade falls & the dead man screams : there are no bars

the cage   the opened mind's a blank   white   sheet of flame

IV.

As long as we are forced to go from black to white, with the first of these abstractions providing something like a point of support for the eye as much as for the brain, we flounder. . .

–Paul Cézanne

If that were really so, in acting for myself I was acting for you too, there is no distinction here, and only an enemy could draw it.

—Franz Kafka

CONTEMPT OF COURT & RUNAWAY CONFESSION: "& NOW THAT YOU ARE MERE EYE. . ."

you'd have to meet her as I did. "Opening & shutting on me. . ." On that day, just at sundown. "Am I as much as. . ." On that night. Hours after sundown. You'd have to meet her. There. Where I did. Having seen her before, many times, even spoken, twice, but never met. Until. "Am I. . ." On that road. "as much as. . ." On that curve in that road on that night. Day. You'd have to slow way down. Headlights off. You'd have had to stop. "Am I as much as. . ." Every single thing you're doing. Where I did. As I did. & meet her, us, then, there in that curve on that day. Night. Us. Then, there'd be three. Follow me. & more. You'd have to watch her. As I did. Do. Move as she did. Does. There. In that night. That sleep. On that road. In that curve. You'd have had to have stopped. Parked. Walked thru barefoot grass. The pond on her back. You'd have to smell the pond at your back. Like I did. See. Like I did. Her. Us. To have met her. What's this? She never saw me approach. Fact is, I didn't. Approach. You'd have had to have followed me. First, I wasn't there. Then, there. Like that. You'd have had to be there like that. And not. Then, there. Like me. Not her. Stop. She wasn't there. The trick. Is. She wasn't there. There were hands in the pond. There was no sound coming from the hands in the pond. No splash. Not a swish. They never surfaced from the pond. Water over thin as the skin on the backs of the hands. Clear waves over wrist bones. Paper thin. The way wrist bones look like closed eyes. Inward. If she wasn't there; then neither the hands. Never broke the surface. That's the eyelid sound of her hands. The movement under the pond. Hands. White hands. The sound of white hands moving under dark water. Thin as unbroken paper. & Eyes. In the air. Close in the air. First, none. Then, all I could see. So close I couldn't count. One, two, three, four, ten eyes. So close I couldn't tell who blinked. All eyes. I felt the wind blink. A pond with no bank. The rims moved. I couldn't see the rims. & no bottom. As if off screen. Back stage. Music from the pit. As if in the margin. Movement beyond the edge. Music in air. A smile. I know there was a face. & hair. Eyes, giveaways. Even today. Right now. [applause] I close my eyes & there they are. Right there. Not an inch. They're not mine. And, a voice: "Save the deaf eyes, what the hell's going to happen to me" Whose voice? Hers. The three of our voices. & movement beyond the rim. Hands make waves. A smile. Hands. Movement underwater. There's a pond at her back. Must have heard me coming. Though I never did. Come. First nothing. Then, there. & no traceable route. No job to do. Just eyes. Not an inch. Right now, there. Before me. Nothing. Then, there. And now. Here. Mine close. Beyond the rim. No sound. White hands & movement beyond the edge. A smile. & pain. Still pain. & music. & movement I can't see. & there's pain. First, nothing. Then, there. Pain beyond the rim. Moves & remains. Beyond the invisible edge. The sound of movement. The sound of water underwater. In my voice she said : "Save the blind ears, I've got a lot of sadness in me" White hands of pain without edge. White hours after sundown with no bottom. A torso rises from the grass. There's nothing beyond the rim. Arms above the head. Imperceptible breasts (mine) & nothing moves above the surface. Wild movement underwater. Waves. Eyes float. I've seen them float before me. Not an inch from the bottom. First not. Then, there. & movement. A torso. But not from place to place. A to B. There. Worse, here. Moved & was still there. Worse, here. Like eyes. Beyond the rim. A torso with grass beyond & a pond behind. Blades of grass tickle her legs, sweat clots in the dirt. All eyes disappear. Not here. Worse, then, not there. & still. & there's my torso. Or, whose? Hands risen. Someone's. White hands (yours) break the surface of the eye. Drops fall. Three, four, ten, they move without a sound. Then merge. A stream in a still pond moves over skin. Ears shattered. Some kind of Socratic passion this is. . . White skin goes away in streaks. Dark streaks blink down my back & onto the ground. They've fallen from hands. Run from leg to leg. Hers to mine. Methodical sweat. You'd have had to have fallen from hands. Thru the surface without a sound. & a cello. Or not. Silence & no cello. Then, there. Or worse. & the eyes appear. Deaf. The whites of these eyes move toward me. Whites hold the darkness at the center. & the darkness at the center moves toward me. There's all the movement I can't see. Streams. Waves travel the pond from where the hands might have tasted the eye. Drops gather drops from where they've fallen to the ground. A torso in the grass. Whose? Moves. Remains. Twists. & eyes. Whiteness holds the darkness & the darkness moves toward me & the darkness at the center of whiteness holds the blackness. The otherwise unavailable, hitherto unalterable, bottom of blackness. Beneath the night that can prove it's the night. Beside the sound of water under hands underwater hands. Her eyes move toward me & look away. Away. Into the sky. Or worse. I've watched eyes move toward me and look away into a sky that can't prove it's not the bottom. I've seen it happen. It has happened. To me & I've seen it. [applause] Eyes away! From my torso to the night sky, proved, & the blackness at the center of darkness opens wide. I've seen eyes look away & I've heard it happen. All I can hear is this happening. You'd have had to have heard it with me. From the inside. Out. O. U. T : out. Hands like silent waves couldn't stop even this. I've heard the blackness overtake the darkness. As the darkness turns from a twist of whiteness & looks away into blackness. A torso moves & remains. Liquids. Blackness overtakes darkness. Whose? Darkness at the center of whiteness moves. Now that's away. Proved. Off center, the blackness opens. Twice at once. I've cursed my brain. An already accursed brain forces all this into one vision. Two into one. I've cut this skin. One into two. Cursed. The eyes stare back. So close & I can't focus & it's my torso that moves in the grass. Remains. Twists. & darkness moves back to the center of whiteness. & blackness closes down. Gives way to darkness. Blackness is, again, a pin-prick pointed at me out of the darkness. . . Now that's away. I didn't have to be this. Me. & eyes I can't count. Two, Six, ten. Huge eyes & not an inch. If there'd been an inch, or if pond-wet fingers found my mouth, I'd be breathing still. In all this time & there's not so much as an inch. There they are now. Reflex & no apologies. For what!? Whiteness, darkness, blindness & blackness. Deafness. & there's movement, away, I can't see. Drops run down the back into Socrates' mouth. Skin. Off the map, a hairpin on a chalk road at midnight. You'd have had to have locked them up. Skin disappears into streams. In front of a pond. Breath opened the pond. The pond at the center of the grass. Torsos move & remain. Twist. Then, there. Eyes inside eyes. Worse. Twisted, remains. Whose? First silence. Hands underwater. Then, there. The broken neck of a cello on its back in the grass. Calm insertions. Arrivals appear. & in your voice she said : "save the thoughtless tongue, excuse me, you've gone red" Nothing approaches. Nothing recedes. You'd have had to have never opened the door. You'd have to never have slammed the door. Teeth marks under the arm'd prove the night's the night. You'd have to forget the door altogether. Shadows bite under the arms. & pleasure searches the bottom. If you'd have seen her. If you'd have seen the darkness hold the blackness & turn away from the torso & the blackness open & swallow the hands & the pond. A black stone dropped into a pool of darkness. Her eye turns away. My torso moves &

remains. Twists. A black wave overtakes the dark. We were there, or worse. Overtaken by black, dark moves into the corner of the white pool. Away. The dark moves. Twists. There's movement in places. & I can't see. There are places beyond places. & I can't move. Beyond the rim. Hands back underwater. [applause] We know them by the sound of a splash we never see. We know them by rings in trees we can't taste. So, we lie about what we haven't seen. Emphatic retractions. Splash. Calm insertions. Lie. Calm retractions & panicked insertions. Panicked retractions. There's a rim beyond the movement. Things remain that can't be seen. The bottom's there. Or worse. Here. Or worse. Sky. The movement can't be seen. Things remain despite retraction. Things one should never have seen. Move & remain. Twist, then there. You thought you'd retracted. Or worse. In fact, you'd plunged beyond the rim. Beyond the movement. Into a kind of falling without moving. You glimpsed movements that remained, you didn't want to see. Or move. Movement beyond the ripple of black thru dark. Calm. Whose? Movement surrounds the hand underwater. There's confusion. What's inserted & what retracted? Deliberate panic. A question of duration? In relation to what? Clocks? [laughter] In relation to a point beyond the invisible rim by which one tells insertion apart from retraction. Beyond the bottomless bottom. Sky. Calm from panic. Fatigue from endurance. A point in a night of wild color. You know, for instance, in bright light heat has a shadow. Whose? Say, a tree falls thru the wind. Say you're on a train. You'd have had to have sat & watched. The two of them. Float, still. Rail ties & stone blur by in a riot. Branches cut the sight of the river. You'd have had to have performed. Experiments with distance. Science. You'd have had to have known the West. On a train. Beyond the blur & the mute cuts thru vision. & thru the realm of circles. The mid-range that revolves. Beyond the blur and past the cut. You'd have had to have focused beyond the cut of poles and branches. Beyond the river. Trees, a fence line revolves. But then up, again, from the circles. The blurred fringe of wheat beyond the rim of your sight. Just beyond that, there's a zone that only moves when you look away. & beyond all that blurs, cuts, spins, lies. There's a point. A tree. An abandoned car. A burnt fort. A broken fence post wrapped in wire. . . You'd have to have known the West. That West. & known beyond known. It. The *only* West. Whose? Gone in a blink. Then, there. You'd have had to have read Balso Snell : the circumference of a circle of unlimited size is a straight line. Have had to have *this* West, Pascal, point, everywhere, tiny to extent it spins but moves not. At all. Known beyond that : known : : a point that doesn't move et al. Here not not here. From whence insertion & panic depart. Thing no empty boots preempt y nothing. Whose? So knock that that. Retraction recedes & hands sweep under the surface. Eyes float [a voice off stage reads from Newton. . . laughter. . . Copernicus . . . jeers. . . Kepler. . .tomatoes]. They'd have to have seen her in the grass. Have they!? They're her eyes. Have they seen her move & remain. Extraspection. A torso disappears in the grass. Twists. Then, there. & worse. Darkness overtaken by blackness in the eye & movement beyond the rim. & if they'd seen it. Have they heard it as I did? Eyes. Two handfuls of mud from the bottom of the pond. Sin thin. A katydid's eyelid. You read it I said it. Tasted, conceived & reported to you now. Explain the plunging, the calm insertion & the vanishing without retraction. The appearing without approaching. The movement beyond the rim. Then, the bottom there. Or worse. Sky. The retraction, away, that plunges thru darkness overtaken by blackness. My torso in the grass. Moves & remains. Twists. Right between the eyes & the eyes narrow as a soft mouth [applause] at the hard edge beyond the rim. Whose? A smile & the calm insertion. & pain that won't appear. Then, there. Won't approach. Then worse. Retraction? [laughter] Exception? [jeers] Come now, come now. Objection! [tomatoes] And, we've left things out. Like the cello. Most often, in these times, we blame it on the cello. Or on machines. &, if all else fails, the devil; and what of friction? There's a point beyond friction from which calm insertion & panicked retraction depart. But, you'd have to have known the West. & felt the grass move beneath your back as mine. Conceived and reported. Blades tickle. Tasted. Palms wet from the grass, you'd have had to have heard her laugh. Red-handed in the West, man, as soon as there's friction. It's never far from the hips. Whose? Never is. Hips beyond the narrowed edge beyond the rim of the eyes. A smile. Once the eyes have narrowed, without, an inch between. Something at the bottom breathes. A banana skin withers faster without the fruit. No matter sun or shade, tree or picked. Faster, wither. Without the fruit. Consult science for the rate. All eyes have hips. The increase. The fact remains. The fact is faster but not as fast as that broken limb wrapped in wire. Or was it a fence post? & there's the fruit of without fruit. Whose? & in the West, without approach, & once there are hips & friction & a cello. There's always something to feel. Calm insertion &, yes, beyond a certain unavailable point in the unapproachable distance within whatever's without. Whomever? Or worse. & beyond what's known of the West. Panicked retraction. Once you've felt the friction, the faster fact is, there's simply no retraction. Plunge within or without; the skin withers. Outno don't say yo-yo. The definition of recoil : post-frictional retraction. In other words, calm insertion. Movement beyond the rim, white hands beneath the surface, blackness over darkness. Away. Then, there. Moves & remains. Once there's friction nothing can appear. Or worse. Twists, tangled. The eyes never retract. Every time one closes, another, inside, opens. The West never sleeps, or wakes. It can't even blink. Hacks on stage mis-quoting Pozzo: "The eyes of the world are a constant quantity." Never you mind experimental performances. Plunges further thru the blackness overtaking darkness. Away. Travels to the corner of whiteness & open. Back. So, need it be said? & if need be then if need be. Whose? Can it be said? Calm insertion. And, if can. There's always must. Or worse. Can't. So go ahead on & must it. But, of course, if there's friction there must. "Am I as much as. . ." The devil's quiver, heat. ". . .as much as" Teeth marks on the hips & narrowing beyond the rim. A smile has its own eye. "Am I as much as. . ." Teeth marks under arms. Truth is : it had nothing to do with what she said– If there's a narrowing there's heat. If friction, the hips. & then the narrowing. " . . .as much as" Calm insertion. & what of light? No, not in this sense, no. Hours ago. Sundown. Though. At night, eyes float & the hands at the bottom of a silent white wave & "Am I as much as being seen?"

V.

only criminals do harm to others without philosophy

  —Robert Musil

 — Forgive pencil, can't find either pen. — Banks & lawyers are killing me. —

  —John Berryman

CROSS-EXAMINATION: AFTER THE READ BACK
THE D.A. GETS ALL GRINCH-COP / BAD-COP

no way either way   no yonder
way to go when your face *is* the fact
thigh bone points & broken flesh-notes
beneath the lapel   silent holes
behind the third rib   we checked out
your lead & sunlight breast   say it
if you rolled   green   down the bright hill
explain open wounds & clean stone

paths   the split bottom lip & blood-prints on the wall

don't worry   we're not really here
to window you son   not to three-
sixty you none   just to owl it
out around the barn a bit   here
to nightwing you   eye to eye like
two .38s   here's an exit
wound in a brushed sole   now don't get
all fan-tailed & feather-handed

oh   we found the sandpaper eye patch

done dredged it deep   ran rusted barbs
& live-wires thru molasses in
the red jar   go on & say it
you've held soft chalk in an open
hand   go on & walk it   round-it
round-the-dog-it   junior   who's gone
all white-eyed behind her eyes   say who
limed her up from ice trays   say who

she melted & how those screams   surprise

AFFIDAVIT FROM THE STEINWAY
BUILDING: BETROTHED & BEREAVED
& NO NEED FOR APPLAUSE

if hindsight's the obliterated song
you'd think a huge black auk
is a risk   if Will de Mouve gets his arms
around you   you just as soon spook
the team with a pistol & wrestle ten
yards of wet rope caught in the wagon
wheel   motherfucker makes up songs
when he fights   remember the jab
rhythm sprung Turn Coat? : "even coat-black

water turns white when it falls   red hot irons

in the bucket   padded cells without walls"
never slept more than a few blinks
when his hands began to ache   found
a gap in a line on a wall
& scraped his blade along the rough
edge of the brick   sang : "some of that mud
over here   or rub ivory on my
hands   snap chalk-lines in the air
& a saffron rain of sands"

I'll give you this : we hated him

most when he smiled   said : times get tight
pays to know what not to feed & what
to starve   a hungry horse sleeps
standing up & leans in for the throat   gravity
explains it   a bared chest draws
dew drops from heavy green   said : one way in

& one way out of Nola's Penthouse   was Nat killed
the lights   said : still ice in the glasses
& pretend your surrounded   fool yourselves snap thin
& remember : the risk is making yourself believe

                              you're better than you are

CONFESSION OF THE PAID EXPERT: FIVE REASONS TO TRY CHILDREN AS ADULTS & ADULTS AS IF THEY'RE ALREADY DEAD

it's why you can't say you need me
to testify beyond the obvious : consider   for one
the coexistence of humans & the abundant supply
of high cliffs   impulse to leap wound in to eggs
frozen in mud beds   to hide   shot out of canons
& pirouettes in the steel eyes of the bald & blazed crowd
of VIPs   say it : you don't need me for this here   try
your own   skull-numb & helium-voiced attraction
to any falling thing   why deny lush waves?   pleasures

owed to must-win losses & irretrievable returns : look :

there she is : corn rowed & powder
puffed   & the one upside down in the dark
knees soaked in blood from the plate of spoiled meat
consider the voices of loved ones : wood rasp
on raw nerves   never mind what I say   stand five
minutes   nude   in cold rain & write it down   verbatim
what you learned about salt & sea wind
up the whetstone slopes of the psyche   stand ten
& you'll trade the last glimpse of the living

for a hole in the snow & a smile sliced under a rock : look :

& here you are   & no need of me   what about
Saturday?   forehead on the elm tree   you
count to twenty   the kids   done digging their graves
decide to hide in piles of leaves   you know
exactly where to look & you know the odds
are you shouldn't ever turn from the tree : look :

& there you are   gone
& the wind's a finger stroke in the hair-thin dark
cut by the red tail of a sight-starved hawk : look :

& there he is : Compte Alphonse de Toulouse-Lautrec

part time falconer   full time costumer   said :
his breed goes straight back to the Crusades
eyes sharp as sunlight crossed up in holy water
wings quiet as blue smoke in a valley of pine
& the smell of burning wormwood : look : there
he is   like all fathers in the hunter's disguise   perched
on his son's deathwatch : look : anywhere
but here   said : that thing I found wasn't my son
anyone   some kind of bright eyed blindness

on a dead-white pillow   hard strike from a poisoned mouth
in a hollow dream   a stranger in someone else's getup looks

back   yellow spots in a shadow   quieter than any retracted fang

ATTORNEY CLIENT PRIVILEGE: DRESS REHEARSAL FOR OUT-OF-KEY TESTIMONY

hear that? it's "The Nearness of You"
there's no one down there, man   hear that?
throw away what you know about
filling empty windows & step round in front
of the voice   go on & open up skin deep
blind spots   no more than handfuls of hoodwink &
sweat-stained starlight   sing soft as white gum
from a broken branch & coal sparks in the spine

from BJ's Glass Cornet   *there's no one there   there's*

no music down there, man   you'll have to swear
you don't see them leaning back & walking uphill
shit   we're all silent crimes to that jury
of stick men   smoke in night's empty sleeve
eyes shuffle across lived lives
like sandy feet on a boarded-up mineshaft
clock watchers 'fraid they'll sniff hot flesh
behind the silent breeze   zero gravity

& weighed in the balan—   hear that?

shadows in a false-fingered hallway   panic follows
scribbled legs up the stairs   they hear
blades of silver rain on flesh-toned grass
finger tips capsized   numb voices
stack the deck from still-born crow's nests
fruit fly rhythms under amber
tongues   hear that?   eight balls spin   blue eyes
snap in silk-lined hands   boo   it's the nearness

of no one   pockets empty & sewn shut from the inside

PLEA BARGAIN OR LOVE CHANT

strict ear   just remember Pink Eyes
routineer in a reading band
with a right hand like the other
side of an oak leaf   Pink Eyes with
midnight on his mind   Robichaux's
hot man in the hole   was the night
they played "Hymn to the Judas Goat"
transposed by ear in minor thirds

heavy shit the deeper you go
more sweat stains than open windows
more than blood songs from the spit valve
you could see songs move in the meat
locker   snouts ringed & frozen shut
rhythm   black jack on an ice flank
this was before Black Star limes for
empty nests   before Xanadu

& Orson Welles on bass   before
biddle bum bum   biddle bum bum
eyes smell the blear   her voice a broke
en china cup from the sewer
wagon   topaz cloud from nine pails
aflame   mouth full of resin smoke
sang darkwet   a 4/4 night job
got her start   round back of the hall

AMICUS BRIEF: FRIENDS WHO KNOW DON'T
ASK   ANYONE WHO ASKS DOESN'T
REALLY WANT TO KNOW ANYONE WHO KNOWS

what?   it's some kind of crime now to be happy
it's someone else who's dead?   everyone's got
an alibi   but how many can use them? :
my client happened to be nowhere
alone   doing absolutely nothing at all
was a time I'd have 6 or 7 alibis
like him on a good Saturday night   ask Judge
Woolsey   what harm in honest sex less a few standards
of punctuation   like any teenage boy dying

to interview a stain on Molly B's sheets   drooled

& mumbled when he come   what was the phrase?   said
it was a Cancer's translation from the Vedic
little fool'd collapse on me   breath hot
in my mouth & gasp   "Evil
does not exist" came to where he'd pay me to hold
myself open with the lights out & whisper it three times
into the mirror over the wash-pot
when I heard he was dead   I won't lie   I saw
what he meant   I can see him now   smooth as a jigsaw

stuck in pine sap   sharp as any maggot dancing

the fine line between live flesh & dead meat   a
zip-locked paladin with a freezer bag
for a stocking cap   ladies in the jury know the type :
fingers barbed like fish hooks & a Dakota blizzard
in his chest   suit & tie by day   at night :
says he wants stow away on a steamer
cause he's convinced his brain's the burning
bush   busts in the door & builds a shrine
to his cranium out of upturned shot glasses

get this : one told me he'd studied death

in translation at a private college
up North   said the smell in the Cedar Bar
is the sound of the Roar that takes the motionless
thing apart   stiffness : fluid
from anything that disappears   had one thing
right: those maggots in the alley are nothing
but milk-spots on God's tonsils   said
he knew a deserted beach
where waves pound black coral back into glass

& sunrises pull salt-wind thru bleached ribs
of a cage made for two   from there it's clear :

10,000 tides sweep like one giant wing

        & each night   fossil albatross rise from the sand

VI.

Logic is doubtless unshakable, but it cannot withstand a man
who wants to go on living.

—Franz Kafka

I armed myself against justice.
I ran away. . .

—Arthur Rimbaud

Nowadays you have to be a scientist if you want to be a killer.

—Vladimir Nabakov

JURY INSTRUCTIONS: JUDGE FOGARTY

no matter who says what   we're not here
about any petty boisterous
outcry   no bid for furious cat
calls from a squash cart   this thing left
bodies scattered   brains scrambled   or not
it's true we got our crying done
at birth   ups or downs   death has to be
mother may I   take one giant step
just as long as you find false footing

in the freefall   long as there's bright blue
under the tongue & bonesteeds gallop
the brain   as long as voices nailed back
behind the wall find you down on one
ruined knee   long as alla breve
whispers back to air cut clean as throats
down around Rampart & Perdido
we rely on standards   need not quote
Brando on a Napoleonic

code shared by all   babies know it : steer
clear & sharpen cold tuning forks ag
ainst the mad pitch of a misfit mind
we all know what happens when mirrors ride
freight trains   still   ain't but a handful ever
played loud & fast enough till the swing
came loose from the scythe   if you believe
what you've heard   go get him a good broom
thirty in the market   take it away

VOLUME TWENTY-ONE: A MURDER
VICTIM'S SUICIDE NOTE
OR   ATTORNEY CLIENT PRIVILEGE

say I swam the blue ledge
off the reef   morning & night
sun up & down   say
I lived to run short
of air & swim under the length
of the dock   what are you
afraid to lie?   never admit
you had the knife to throw   say
you only skipped stones
for the pools of fire at sundown
say : rotator cuff
walk to the end   count to fifty

& hurl it straight down   story is :

I came up for breath

you *do* know how to lie?
I love you   lie on me
forget those stellar stair-steps
"Seraphic Light"
from a glimpse of underwater
hair   someone spilled
motor oil   a squid down
my back & a trail of ink
remember all the lies
all the satin envelopes
slipped under blood-streaked fire doors

say we're weightless   pinholes
too pink to sleep with   the paper skull of

                              a fetal bat buried in the ash

PROSECUTION'S CLOSING ARGUMENT: WARNING: OBJECTS IN MIRROR ARE CLOSER THAN THEY APPEAR IN RETROSPECT

someone wake me up before I start to dream
he's not still dead   people : "chaos is the score"
but for us & those like us   the Verdict's liable to be death
to our lost & found rhythm of real sentences   as for
Arguments   face it   all we have is our hopes for the wan-beef
jerky of American skin tone & whatever else we can wet slap
on the silent seam in a hollow needle   you're looking at him   a collapsed
vein in the long   withered arm of the law   let's us presently
rehearse the facts : we tried to hold him   a bailiff's finger in each pocket

bailiff : show the finger to the court   ok   now the other one

recall the voice from the alley :
grab two handfuls   cumuli   & what need had he of a weapon?

haven't we all slept in unmade beds under plate-glass sheets
how many here haven't lifted bloody prints from a miracle
that stabbed you in the back   witnesses saw the eye itself open wide & fly
from the trestle   look at him   there   slave to the moon-grazed
crest of a nightwave a.k.a. Prisoner Emeritus
never once left his stoop without his VIP pass
to the bottom of the moat   every third day spent mounted
by the spirit of grift & graft   sacrificed
another lump of silk-strewn meat you & I'd never weigh

against dust on a minnow & a silver hook in a motionless pool

the trap is that bright light in his gullet   don't listen
to him say it   remember only what he said   picture
that freezer drawer full of gangrene   forget he said the song
couldn't be sung but so fast   use *your* tempo   no
excuses   no matter first-born to red beads in an iron skillet
this is America   don't we all owe it all to the diastole
& systole of disaster   what's all the froufrou?   copper tongues
gone to verdigris   friends   he'd cut all the flagpoles
in half & hand *you* the axe   wait : motion : for a short recess

go   splash water on your face   get clean again   leave things you're afraid of

behind   the sight of your thoughts   throttled   akimbo on the tile

SCIRE FACIAS: DR TCHICAI, ALIAS, ER FROM BENEATH BEYOND

nothing in his throat but a quick
swig of witch wind & miracle
cure   swore a blood oath to repeat
offenders   a falconer &
two brigands   this before Talaat
& the Young Turks got old   razor-
lipped & one-time troubadour   sang
a lax prayer for the night blind &

flipped a one-sided coin in his
brain   took a chorus & broke blood
vessels in the blank slate   said lets
name the trio of fallacies
talent   duty   & amusement
blind for this life   was Thamyris chose
freckles on an egg   said never
mind nightingales held for Ransom

Ajax   at the corner   headed
back off the edge   said lions steal
suits for heroes   Odysseus
dead for the moment   said   when he's alive
he gets jelly on a roll &
won't touch the jar   said *bo-ring!*   said
if you'd choose to do it all again
then there's no point in living at all

VOLUME 22: POTSHOTS AT A SON-IN-LAW

beneath the syrupy soundtracks
we've pulverized   best
friends mercy-murdered   always
off stage & by
chalk-faced choruses of regret
that's what I had to lie about
the deep bruise   & who'd believe the faces
that hover off the tip of my nose
I still laugh every time   a real laugh : that
city sidewalks may stop nothing
butbutbut   something has to at least delay
the trampling of faces into mud

femurs cracked over ruts   the choking on dust

up off hard-packed dirt   fear & energy :
5 February 1944   Leone
Ginzburg tortured
to death in Regina Coeli
according to Pavese   26 June
Aristotle's aesthetics :
top two ways to fail a tragedy:
1) "one knows and kills the victim"; or 2)
"the victim's identity is known
but the killing is prevented at the last moment"

a toast : here's to the end of experience
clueless neighbors having replaced
everybody else   recall : he loved to laugh   kept to himself

the first crack   they say
is unbelievably loud
but   there's a limited edition
illustrated manual
shows how to use mass transit
how to pretend you're going to sleep
standing up   how to forget
the foot that feels for the ground
& modus vivendi akin
to daylight on love in a ripe
field of wheat : monks engrave
blades & carve errors of blood in sacred dust

what about one that's both
or neither   a girl from Baltimore
fought till death without a glance
to win   a willow smoulders
on stage & too thin to sweat   she lays waste
to another ice patch & a pool of burnt
bliss at La Scala in '58

beaded black silk draped over starlight
& neck gone to nape the color
of a Tuscan sundown   she sings
"I don't want to cry. . ."

& off mic: "tear out the window—   Mal
wide the chord open & empty
enough till I can sing this fucking song"

CLOSING ADDRESS TO THE JURY
THE DEFENSE RESTS: "FOUR
PIECES IN THE FORM OF A PEAR"

before you taste that avalanche
of saucers & trail Virginie Lebeau thru
la Glacière & la Santé   past the executioner's
square   thru the crowd gathered
around the corner from dawn   gait
metered   Gymnopediste   a pendulum swings
over a paper sack full of peach
pits   either carry your own hammer
or fill his pockets on the sly

with 27 new masks for mute wood   which
one are you?   the surly drunk or the empty Parisian

gutter   walk right past Man Ray
in Montparnasse   hell bent
to show Kiki how to walk dead
ahead into winter rain   Lebeau's cousin
   Narcisse   left hand astir
in his coat pocket   cut in & said : what you want trouble?
the trouble with trouble up here
in the village: it's like if death fucked life
& gave birth to twins   throw in the outfits

& a drink on the house   & none anymore   can tell them apart

before you go & lick that sharp shred of the fallen
saucer   trail the avalanche past the sisters
who sell themselves to the sunrise
at the executions   ask him when   ask
the first time he found himself between a ghost & whore
at a hanging & when he began to lean   ever-slightly
toward the noise   the new Trinity : "every time you hear a bell
someone comes   someone pays & someone dies"   ask
Braque why he ran his hands thru the dead

scales of everything in '26   by then   they'd found
piles back of soiled drapes & read Lebeau's undelivered

lecture on the contents of hand soap   "mostly sweat
& human waste. . ."   he knew nobody he wanted
to have the stack of pumice stones   at auction
they outbid themselves on torn sheets
of failure & went home thinking clean   he knew no one
peels a pocket full
of overripe bananas just to risk the white
night sky won't   one day soon
      pull its blue fist from the mouth of that little

sun-brown boy   there at the keys   astraddle Manuel de Falla's lap

JURY DELIBERATIONS FOR THE LATECOMER:
SELECTED QUERIES & APHORISMS
OF ISIDORO CAPDEPÓN FERNANDEZ

if I take the five talc fingers
from curlicues lost on your belly   would you
please let me know if I should be liking
this?   webbed toes on demand wasn't even
close   had to be two lead feet tangled in
shadows of white lilies at the bottom
of the pond callused thumbs flick tin keys
& a spit-shined trance walks the salt-flat plane
of bone   save sunrises

easy over & the rest of your impossible

tasks for fringe in the hole   the plaintiff's pockets
filled with hot stones   earth that deep don't stay
dry in the dark   lives crumbled & blown off
a hard-slapped palm   chin behind a shoulder
if you want pick up sticks & the nimble
night   the hollow-rib rhythm
of the concave dog in your dreams   stop leaning
the knee-high ladder on the empty moon   don't pretend
that fool's shrieks from the cellar

won't come again   no   the door's not bowed beneath

steel-eyed raindrops washed off the last greenback
in a duck's brain   "hurl'em if you got'em"
frozen effigies in the flypaper
pit   recall Argus   both arms of eyes asleep   origin
of the phrase : bored to death   sheer the skin
swept of its curtains & watch the slate sky
turn thick as a leach hooked in the blood-hole
burn the burnt-blind eye   again & again
until it's undaunted   the invisible   shattered

thing that you just had to know   would be whole

Soft Volcano

Libby Burton

saturnalia books

Distributed by University Press of New England
Hanover and London

Saturnalia Books
105 Woodside Rd.
Ardmore, PA 19003
info@saturnaliabooks.com

ISBN: 978-0-9980534-8-6
Library of Congress Control Number: 2017957996

Book Design by Robin Vuchnich
Printing by McNaughton & Gunn

Author Photo: Alexandra Levin

Distributed by:
University Press of New England
1 Court Street
Lebanon, NH 03766
800-421-1561

For publishing poems from this collection, sometimes in different iterations, my deepest gratitude to the editors of the *Atlas Review, Denver Quarterly, Guernica, Inscape, Juked, La Jovea, North American Poetry Review, Tin House, Western Humanities Review* and the *Brooklyn Poets Anthology*.

For their support, kindness, generosity, humor, and big-heartedness, I would love to thank my fantastic family—Jeffrey, Nancy, and Julie Burton—and my husband, Aaron Berman. For their endless insight, fraternity, and immutable talent, which they shared with me, I am grateful to Ricardo Maldonado, Wil Lobko, and Maud Poole, as well as Sarah V. Schweig and Alexandra Wilder. Thank you to Adrienne Trinka, for so so much. And to my wonderful teachers: Lisa Russ Spaar, first and foremost, as well as Karen Kevorkian, Charles Wright, Rita Dove, Marie Howe, Brenda Shaunessey, Lucie Brock-Broido, and Cornelius Eady. Thank you to Christopher Salerno, Henry Israeli, Robin Vuchnich, Ross Gay, and everyone at Saturnalia.